BENJAMIN FRANKLIN

Printer, Inventor, Statesman

BENJAMIN FRANKLIN

Printer, Inventor, Statesman
A FIRST BIOGRAPHY

by DAVID A. ADLER

illustrated by Lyle Miller

Holiday House / New York

IMPORTANT DATES

1706	Born on January 17 in Boston.
1718–1723	Worked in his brother's print shop.
1722	"Silence Dogood" letters published in the *New England Courant*.
1728	Opened his own print shop in Philadelphia.
1729	Bought and began to publish the *Pennsylvania Gazette*.
1730	Married Deborah Read on September 1.
1730 or 1731	Son William born. (The exact date is unknown.)
1731	Set up a circulating library in Philadelphia, perhaps the first in America.
1732–1758	Published *Poor Richard's Almanack*.
1732	Son Francis born. He died four years later of smallpox.
1736–1751	Clerk of General Assembly of Pennsylvania.
1743	Daughter Sarah born on August 31.
1752	In June, flew a kite in a thunderstorm and proved that lightning is electricity.
1753	Awarded the Copley Medal for his experiments with electricity.
1753–1774	Postmaster of the American colonies.
1754	At Albany Convention, submitted plan for union of colonies.
1764–1775	Represented the American colonies in England.
1771	Wrote the first part of his autobiography; began the second part in 1784.
1775	Elected delegate to Second Continental Congress.
1776	Signed Declaration of Independence.
1776–1785	Represented the United States in France.
1782	Helped write peace treaty with England.
1785–1788	President of Pennsylvania Assembly.
1787	Delegate to Constitutional Convention.
1790	Died on April 17 in Philadelphia.

CONTENTS

1. *One Sunday Morning on Milk Street*

IN 1706, the year Benjamin Franklin was born, Boston was the largest city in the thirteen American colonies. More than ten thousand people lived there in some three thousand houses. There were one hundred streets, lanes, and alleys. Among them were King and Queen streets (the colonies were still loyal to the king and queen of England), School Street, Winter and Summer Streets, Milk Street, and Water Street.

On Sunday morning, January 17, 1706, Boston's one hundred streets, lanes, and alleys were covered with snow. Just three days before, a fierce storm had hit the city. The snow was so deep that one man was actually lost in it and died. On that Sunday, in a four-room house on Milk Street, Josiah Franklin saw his fifteenth child and tenth son born. Later that day, Josiah carried the baby across the street to the Old South Church, where he was baptized.

Benjamin was named for his father's brother. The older Benjamin Franklin had a tragic life. By 1706 his wife had died and so had nine of his ten children. Lonely Uncle Benjamin often went to church with paper and pen and wrote down every word

of the sermons. He had many volumes of these handwritten speeches and he read them over and over. For a few years Uncle Benjamin lived in Boston with the Franklins, and he took a special interest in his namesake.

Josiah Franklin, the baby's father, was born in England. In 1683, when he was twenty-five, he came to the colonies with his wife, Anne, and their three children.

Josiah was a dyer of cloth, but in Boston, where colonists were struggling to make a living, the color of cloth was not important. So Josiah became a soap- and candlemaker. He did a brisk business. Even in colonial Boston, people needed soap, and during the long, dark winter nights, they needed plenty of candles.

Altogether, Josiah and Anne Franklin had seven children—Elizabeth, Samuel, Hannah, Josiah, Anne, Joseph, and another Joseph. Both sons named Joseph died soon after they were born. Josiah's wife, Anne, died, too, in 1689, while giving birth to the second Joseph.

Josiah Franklin was thirty-one years old. He had five young children and not enough time to take care of them, his house, and his soap and candle shop. Within several months he married Abiah Folger, a strong, hearty twenty-two-year-old woman from nearby Nantucket. She took care of Josiah's five children and bore Josiah ten more—John, Peter, Mary, James, Sarah, Ebenezer, Thomas, Benjamin, Lydia, and Jane. Benjamin was the fifteenth of Josiah's seventeen children.

Josiah Franklin was a talented man with varied interests. Besides being a dyer, soap- and candlemaker, he played the violin, sang songs, drew pictures, and was handy with a hammer. He was a good listener and a respected man in the community. His son Benjamin wrote of him, "I remember well his being frequently visited by leading people, who consulted him for his opinion in affairs of the town or the church he belonged to, and showed a good deal of respect for his judgment and advice."

Josiah also liked to experiment. Once he took herring eggs from one river and carried them to another. Josiah waited and watched until the second river filled up with herring, just like the first.

Young Benjamin Franklin liked to experiment, too. He tried using paddles to help him swim faster, but they tired him out. He tried flying a kite while he swam and that worked better. He found that in a good wind, the kite pulled him across the water.

Even before Benjamin went to school, he was considered especially smart. Soon after he learned to talk, he taught himself to read. It became his favorite pastime, but often young Benjamin had difficulty finding something new to read. In Boston in the eighteenth century, books were scarce. Benjamin read mostly volumes of ministers' sermons.

Josiah was pleased to see his son reading sermons, since he had planned a life of church service for Benjamin. It was proper to give one-tenth of your earnings to the church. In the same spirit, Josiah planned that Benjamin, his tenth son, would go into the ministry.

At eight Benjamin was sent to the Boston Latin School. There Josiah wanted him to prepare to enter Harvard to study theology. But Josiah soon gave up this idea. With so many children he couldn't afford to send Benjamin to an expensive school for more than a year. He also realized that Benjamin would not make a good minister. He was not very devout. When his family said grace at meals, Benjamin was impatient. One day, in the

family's storeroom, he suggested that his father simply say grace once, over a cask of salted meat, and not waste time on it at each meal before the meat was served.

After Josiah took Benjamin out of Boston Latin School, he enrolled him in a school for writing and arithmetic. Benjamin did well in writing, but he wrote later in his autobiography, "I failed in the arithmetic and made no progress in it."

At age ten, Benjamin's father removed him from school altogether and made him work in his soap and candle shop. There Benjamin cut wicks for the candles, filled the dipping molds, helped look after the shop, and went on errands.

Even though Benjamin was no longer in school, he continued to learn from the books he read and from firsthand experience. When he was seven he bought a whistle, and learned the value of money. His brothers and sisters laughed at him and said he had paid too much for it. Benjamin cried. He was sorry he had spent the money. Years later he wrote, ''A penny saved is two pence clear,'' ''Get what you can and what you get hold,'' and ''Save what you may, no morning sun lasts the whole day.'' During the rest of his life, Benjamin was careful not to spend more money than necessary on anything.

He learned about honesty after fishing for minnows with his friends. They took some stones from a building site. They piled them up and stood on top of them so they could fish and still keep their feet dry. Benjamin was caught and forced to return the stones. He wrote later that his father, ''convinced me that nothing was useful which was not honest.'' He wrote elsewhere, ''He that gets all he can honestly, and saves all he gets will certainly become rich.'' But perhaps honesty is not the only lesson he learned that day. He also wrote, ''Keep your mouth wet and feet dry.''

Josiah Franklin's soap and candle shop was hot and filled with bad odors. Benjamin hated working there. He was a good swimmer and knew how to manage a boat. Josiah was afraid that he would run off to sea, as Benjamin's older half-brother Josiah had done.

The elder Josiah Franklin took Benjamin on walks to see bricklayers, blacksmiths, cabinetmakers, roofers, brass workers, and coopers at work. He hoped Benjamin would choose a

trade. He didn't, but his father's efforts were not wasted. From watching the craftsmen, Benjamin learned to do little fix-it jobs at home.

At last Josiah decided his son would be a cutler, a maker of scissors and knives. He sent him to Samuel, the one surviving child of Uncle Benjamin. But when Samuel asked to be paid to train his cousin, Josiah took Benjamin home again.

Next, Josiah decided that since his son loved to read, Benjamin would become a printer. Benjamin's older brother, James, had just returned from England with type and a printing press. He was setting up a shop on Queen Street, next door to the jail. Benjamin was made his apprentice. He signed a contract to work until he was twenty-one in exchange for a room, food to eat, some clothing, training as a printer, and a little pay during his last year of service.

2. *Benjamin and Mrs. Silence Dogood*

AT AGE TWELVE, Benjamin dressed for work as a printer's apprentice in a coarse shirt, leather pants, and high, blue wool socks. He worked ten, twelve, and sometimes fourteen hours a day, sweeping, keeping the fire in the fireplace going, running errands, sorting and setting type, inking and running the press. After the workday was done, Benjamin stayed up late and read. He also sometimes skipped church on Sunday so he could read some more.

One book he read, *The Way to Health, Long Life, and Happiness,* convinced him to stop eating meat and fish, to become a vegetarian. Until then James had been paying for Benjamin to get his meals at a boardinghouse. Benjamin asked his brother to give him just half the money the meals had cost him. He would buy his own food. From then on, at mealtime, Benjamin stayed in the print shop to eat and read. His dinner was some bread or biscuits, water, and a handful of raisins or a tart from the bakery. Benjamin used what was left from the money James gave him for food to buy more books.

There was another book-loving young man working nearby, John Collins, and he became a close friend of Benjamin. They spoke often, and almost as often, they argued. Once they argued about whether or not women could study and learn as well as men. John Collins said they couldn't. Benjamin said they could.

The two friends didn't see each other for a while after that, so Benjamin wrote his opinions on the matter. He sent them to John Collins who wrote back. Several letters passed between them. One day Benjamin's father found the letters and spoke to his son about them. He attacked his son's manner of writing, rather than the content of the letters. Benjamin wrote later that his father said he "fell far short in elegance of expression." Benjamin vowed to improve. He did, of course. With *Poor Richard's Almanack,* which he began to write and publish later in 1732, Benjamin Franklin became America's best-selling author.

Benjamin did not get along with his older brother James, who sometimes beat him. The two brothers would take their arguments to their father, who usually sided with Benjamin. Benjamin wrote later in his autobiography, "I was either generally in the right or else a better pleader."

In 1719 James was hired to print the *Boston Gazette,* a weekly newspaper, one of the first in America. He printed forty issues of the paper. Then the work was given to another printer, but James was not out of the newspaper business. He decided to write and print one of his own. He named it the *New England Courant.*

The newspaper was one sheet, printed on both sides. It contained a list of ships arriving and leaving Boston Harbor, some local news, and news from the colonies and Europe. There were also letters and essays from James's friends. The friends used made-up names such as Tom Tram, Ichabod Henroost, Tabitha Talkative, Abigail Afterwit, and Homespun Jack. They made fun of the fancy people of Boston and wrote of the charms of the young women there.

Then, one morning in 1722, a letter was found on the floor of the printshop. During the night someone had pushed it under the door. It was signed *Mrs. Silence Dogood,* and in it she wrote about herself and what she thought of others.

Silence Dogood wrote that she had been born on a ship on its way from England to the colonies. Her father had died on board and she had been raised by her widowed mother. Silence Dogood worked for a minister. They had married and now had three children. Later the minister, her husband, died.

Silence Dogood made fun of women's fashions and of wealthy young men who wasted their time at college. She proposed that women be educated, and that there be some insurance to help poor widows.

The letters were popular, but they weren't from Silence Dogood. There was no such person. They were from sixteen-year-old Benjamin Franklin. After penning fourteen Dogood letters, he stopped writing them. Someone wrote to him through the newspaper, "Are you asleep or on a journey and cannot write?" That's when Benjamin told James that he was the author of the letters.

James wasn't proud of his brother's good writing. He was angry. He felt the boy was just an apprentice and had no business thinking of himself as a writer.

The *New England Courant* often criticized Samuel Shute, the English governor of the Massachusetts Bay Colony. James Franklin was thrown in jail twice for offending the governor, and both times Benjamin was left in charge of the newspaper. The second time, in 1723, it was ruled that anything James published had to be approved first by the secretary of the colony.

James did not want to submit everything he wrote to someone else before he could print it, so he found a way around the ruling. He quit as publisher and named his brother Benjamin as his replacement. Benjamin had not offended the governor, and with him as publisher, the newspaper was no longer subject to review. Of course, to do that James had to first tear up his brother's contract as his apprentice.

James planned to keep control of the newspaper and therefore of Benjamin. But without the contract, Benjamin began to think of leaving. James knew it, so he spoke to the other printers in Boston and told them not to hire the boy. That didn't stop seventeen-year-old Benjamin Franklin. Late at night, on September 25, 1723, he and his friend John Collins boarded a ship bound for New York.

It was a three-day boat trip and, while on board, the sailors caught some fish. Benjamin, still a vegetarian, was upset to see the fish being caught, killed, and eaten. But he was also hungry. The smell of the fish frying tempted him. As he watched the fish being cut open, he saw small fish being taken out of the bigger fishes' stomachs. Well, Benjamin reasoned, if one fish can eat another, then he could eat them both.

New York in the 1720s was a smaller city than Boston, and Benjamin went to its one printing shop. The owner, William Bradford, didn't need help, so he directed Benjamin to Philadelphia where his son, Andrew, had a print shop.

Benjamin took two boat trips and walked a long distance before finally arriving in Philadelphia. The first boat trip was quite an adventure. A drunken Dutch passenger fell into the water and might have drowned if quick-thinking Benjamin Franklin hadn't reached down, grabbed the man by his hair, and dragged him aboard.

Benjamin reached Philadelphia on a Sunday. The people were dressed in their finest clothes. Benjamin was wearing work clothes and his pockets were stuffed with extra shirts and socks. He was tired, hungry, and only had one Dutch dollar. He met a boy carrying bread and asked him for directions to the bakery. When he got there, he asked for three pennies worth of bread and got three great, puffy rolls. He walked up Market Street with one large roll under each arm, while eating the third.

Benjamin passed the house of Mr. and Mrs. John Read. Their daughter Deborah, Benjamin Franklin's future wife, looked out and saw him. She thought he looked quite awkward and ridiculous.

Benjamin was poor then, but kindhearted. After eating one roll, he was no longer hungry. He gave the other two to a woman and her child who were waiting by the water to board a boat.

Benjamin went to Andrew Bradford's shop, but found no work there. Bradford directed him to a new print shop. It belonged to Samuel Keimer, who hired him. Benjamin boarded in the nearby house owned by Mr. John Read.

The governor of Pennsylvania, Sir William Keith, stopped by the print shop one day and complained that the printing done in Philadelphia was wretched. He offered to help Benjamin set up his own shop, give him colony business, and do everything he could to make him a success.

Benjamin sailed to London to buy printing equipment. He didn't have much money, so he planned to borrow what he would need to pay for it. The sellers would surely trust that he would repay the loans because there would be letters of credit from Sir William Keith, governor of the Pennsylvania Colony.

Letters from the governor were brought aboard and given to the captain. After the boat had crossed the ocean, Benjamin was finally able to sort through them. There was no letter of credit. A distraught Benjamin Franklin told a friend he made on board about the missing letters. The friend laughed at the idea that the governor would send such a letter. First, the man was not at all dependable. Second, he didn't have any credit himself. Benjamin had no choice when he arrived in London but to work again in someone else's print shop.

Benjamin enjoyed his time in London. He went to plays, concerts, and found a great many books to read. He even wrote a philosophical booklet of his own, *A Dissertation on Liberty and Necessity, Pleasure and Pain*. While he was away, he sent just one letter to the woman he was courting in Philadelphia, Deborah Read. He told her that he would not be returning soon.

After more than a year, Benjamin headed back to Philadelphia to work for Samuel Keimer. Benjamin was the most skilled printer in the shop. He supervised and trained the other workers, and Keimer paid him well. But once the others were trained, Keimer didn't need Franklin so badly and wanted to cut his salary. Franklin quit. He and Hugh Meredith, another of Keimer's workers, set up a shop of their own. Benjamin did most of the work and Meredith, with money from his father, paid the bills.

3. *Early to Bed and Early to Rise*

In 1728, at age twenty-two, Benjamin Franklin had his own print shop and he meant to make it a success. He not only was serious and worked hard, but he made sure the people of Philadelphia knew it. He dressed plainly and was careful not to be seen standing about and talking. He never went fishing or shooting and only occasionally read a book in public. Sometimes, to show that he was not above doing any of the work necessary for his shop, he pushed a wheelbarrow piled high with paper through the streets of Philadelphia. He also paid his bills promptly, so people were happy to do business with him.

In 1729 Franklin and Meredith bought a newspaper from Samuel Keimer, the *Pennsylvania Gazette*. Franklin filled it with news of politics, fires, accidents, disease, and death, as well as his well-written essays. The newspaper became popular and profitable.

Franklin and Meredith worked together for about one year, but Meredith was not very industrious and not a good printer. He preferred to spend his time drinking at a local tavern. With loans from two friends, Franklin bought Meredith's half of the print shop and newspaper. In 1732 an advertisement in the newspaper announced that a new almanac, *Poor Richard's Almanack*

by Richard Saunders, would soon be published. In the first edition, Poor Richard informed his readers that he wrote the book because his wife could no longer tolerate his idleness. But the author of the almanac was not idle at all, and he was not Richard Saunders. The author was Benjamin Franklin.

Franklin published one almanac each year for the next twenty-five years. In each was a calendar, predictions of the weather, times of sun and moon risings and settings, high and low tides, recipes, advice, and bits of information. The books also contained proverbs, including, ''Nothing but money is sweeter than honey,'' ''Fish and visitors stink in three days,'' ''Early to bed and early to rise, makes a man healthy, wealthy, and wise,'' and

"The sleeping fox catches no poultry. Up! Up!" With sales of ten thousand copies a year, *Poor Richard's Almanack* was the best-selling book in the colonies.

Benjamin Franklin had more than just business on his mind. In 1730 or 1731, the exact date is unknown, he had a son named William. History does not record the name of the boy's mother, but whoever she was, Benjamin was not married to her. It was time, he knew, to settle down. He began, again, to court Deborah Read.

After the time Benjamin had last showed interest in her, Deborah had married a man named John Rogers. Rogers became deeply in debt and some say he was married to another woman in London. He ran off, leaving Deborah behind. John Rogers's whereabouts and condition were unknown.

Franklin wrote later in his autobiography that he took Deborah "to wife September 1st, 1730," but it was not a church wedding, nor a wedding at all. They began living together and had what is known as a common-law marriage. Benjamin's son William lived with them and so did Deborah's widowed mother.

Both Benjamin and Deborah were careful with their money. They set a simple table and had no servants. Franklin described his furniture as "of the cheapest." He wrote later of his wife, "She proved a good and faithful helpmate, assisted me much by attending the shop; We throve together, and we have mutually endeavored to make each other happy."

Benjamin and Deborah Franklin had two children together. A son named Francis was born on October 20, 1732. He died four years later from smallpox. At the time, the use of vaccines was still not widely accepted. It was considered dangerous, but Benjamin deeply regretted not having had Francis inoculated. A daughter named Sarah was born on August 31, 1743. She lived to adulthood.

Benjamin Franklin was not a very religious man. He belonged to the local Presbyterian church, but he seldom went to its services. He considered the minister's speeches "dry, uninteresting, and unedifying." Nonetheless, he wrote in his autobiography, he never doubted "the existence of the Diety; that He made the world and governed it by His Providence."

The Sundays he skipped church became studying-reading days for Franklin, and he read plenty. He and some friends formed a library, perhaps the first in America. Each member paid to join and paid a yearly fee as well. The money was used to buy books for the collection. Beginning in 1733, Benjamin began teaching himself to read books in other languages, too—French, Italian, Spanish, and Latin.

Benjamin also formed a secret discussion group, the Junto, which met on Friday evenings. Their debates were to be ''in the sincere spirit of inquiry after truth.'' They discussed such questions as, is it proper to put a diseased, yet innocent, man to death to stop an epidemic? Should a bad law be obeyed? Who would make a better friend, a wise, good, poor man or a rich man who was neither wise nor good?

Benjamin Franklin wrote in his autobiography, ''I spent no time in taverns.'' He was probably too busy. He was clerk of the Pennsylvania General Assembly from 1736 to 1751 and a member of the Assembly for thirteen years after that.

He was postmaster of Philadelphia and later postmaster general of the colonies. Franklin also set up the first fire company in Philadelphia and the first police force in the colonies. In 1741 he advertised a new stove he had designed, the Franklin stove, which did a better job of heating a house than a fireplace and used less fuel. He didn't take out a patent on the stove. He didn't want to make a profit from helping people keep warm. Franklin and some friends set up an academy in 1751 that later became the University of Pennsylvania.

Benjamin Franklin also spent time trying to improve himself. In 1733 he made a chart of thirteen virtues that he wanted to practice. He paid ''strict attention'' each week to working on one of the virtues—temperance, silence, order, resolution, frugality, industry, sincerity, justice, moderation, cleanliness, tranquillity, chastity, or humility. Each time he failed in one of those virtues, he placed a little black spot on his chart. He considered himself full of faults, but he wrote in his autobiography, ''I had the satisfaction of seeing them diminish.''

4. *Join or Die*

In 1748 when Benjamin Franklin was forty-two years old, he retired from business. He was a wealthy man and he had a great many interests beyond making money. He wanted to experiment, to dabble in science, especially in electricity.

His experiments with electricity were dangerous. One year he planned to kill his Christmas turkey with an electric shock. After a great flash and a large noise—a crack like the sound of a gunshot—Benjamin Franklin lay on the floor. He was knocked unconscious. But he had success, too, with his experiments. In 1749, using lead and glass, he made the first battery.

In June 1752, he conducted his famous kite and lightning experiment. He made a kite out of silk and two sticks. From the top of the kite, he attached a wire to act as a lightning catcher. To the string he attached a silk ribbon and a key. His son William flew the kite in the midst of a storm. Lightning hit the wire. Benjamin Franklin touched the key and felt a spark. He had proved that lightning is electricity.

Next Franklin made use of his discovery. He invented the lightning rod. In most houses the rods, when struck, carried electricity into the ground where it would do no harm. But this was not true in Benjamin Franklin's house. In his house, the rod led to two bells with a brass ball between them. When lightning hit the rod, sparks flew, making the bells ring.

Franklin experimented with ants, too. He hung a clay pot filled with molasses from a string nailed to the ceiling. In the pot was a single ant. Franklin waited and watched. When the ant had eaten the molasses, it left the pot, climbed the string to the ceiling, and then climbed down the wall. Shortly after that a parade of ants found their way to the molasses, because, Franklin was sure, the first ant somehow told them where it was. Ants, he concluded, had a way of communicating with each other.

Franklin invented bifocal eyeglasses, made a chair with a seat that folded to became a stepladder, and a long arm pole that could grab things from high shelves. He also invented the armonica, later called the harmonica, a musical instrument made of glass. He liked to play with numbers and made magic squares, squares subdivided into smaller boxes, each with a different number inside. The magic happened when someone added the numbers in any horizontal, vertical, or diagonal row. The answer was always the same.

Benjamin Franklin was awarded honorary degrees from Harvard College, Yale College, Oxford University, and the College of William and Mary. He was elected to the French Academy of Sciences and in 1753 received the Copley Medal from the Royal Society of London. He was one of the leading scientists of his generation.

In 1754 the French and Indian War, a war over land between the French and the British, broke out. It was the fourth war in America between the two countries since 1689. Some Indians fought on the side of the French and others on that of the British. American colonists fought alongside the British.

Benjamin Franklin wrote in his newspaper, the *Pennsylvania Gazette,* how the French were readying for war. He urged the colonies to fight together against them and drew his famous cartoon of a snake cut into eight pieces with these words beneath it, ''JOIN, or DIE.'' He was sent by the Pennsylvania Assembly to the Albany Congress where he proposed that the colonies join together ''for defense and other general purposes.'' The plan

was approved by the delegates to the convention, but not by the assemblies of the colonies. Even the Pennsylvania Assembly voted against it.

The Pennsylvania Colony was built on land given in 1681 by King Charles II of England to William Penn. Penn sold parcels of land to colonists. In 1757 the Pennsylvania Assembly sent Franklin to London. His mission was to petition the king to tax the Penn family. The colonists needed the money to help them pay to maintain their army and defend the colony from the French.

Franklin and his son William, who would be his secretary, traveled to New York. They planned to board a ship to London, but French warships were thought to be nearby. They had to wait, which was difficult for Franklin as he was not used to being idle. He wrote to Deborah, ''This tedious state of uncertainty and long waiting has almost worn out my patience. I know not when I have spent time so uselessly.'' He also wrote, ''I left my best spectacles on the table. Please to send them to me.''

The Franklins finally sailed. At sea their boat was chased by the French, and was almost shipwrecked. Franklin was greatly relieved when they arrived safely in London in July 1757.

London, with its 750,000 people, was the largest city in Europe. Franklin wanted to be accepted by the upper class. Soon after he arrived, he bought silver shoe and knee buckles, new shoes and shirts, a dress sword with a belt to hold it, spectacles, wigs, a watch, candlesticks, china, and a carriage.

In 1760 Franklin won for the Pennsylvania Assembly the right for England to tax the Penns, but he remained in London for two more years. In October 1761, he attended the coronation of King George III.

An American newspaper, the *Boston News-Letter,* lauded the new king for his wisdom, piety, and the respect and love he showed to his mother. It described the king's almost simple life. He lit his own lamp, dressed himself, and ate a crust of bread and drank a glass of water for supper. Franklin called him, "Our virtuous young king." Within fifteen years Benjamin Franklin's tone would change. He would sign the Declaration of Independence declaring the colonies independent of this virtuous king.

5. *Liberty*

BENJAMIN FRANKLIN returned to the colonies in 1762, but remained there for only two years. They were busy years, as he was still postmaster general. He traveled to post offices throughout the colonies and looked for ways to improve mail service. He also visited his son William who returned from London in 1763. By then William was married and the royal governor of New Jersey.

The French and Indian War had ended, but there was still trouble with the Indians. In the spring of 1763 there was a Native American revolt, "Pontiac's Conspiracy," in which Indians overran many British forts east of the Mississippi River. Then, on December 14, 1763, a group of Native Americans, among them children, women, and the elderly, were killed by the "Paxton Boys," Pennsylvanian frontier settlers. After the slaughter, the settlers marched toward Philadelphia to kill the Native Americans living there. Franklin gathered soldiers and guns. He met the Paxton Boys and convinced them to leave without violence.

A few weeks later Franklin wrote about the massacre and against prejudice. "If an Indian injures me, does it follow that I may revenge that injury on all Indians? . . . The only crime of these poor wretches seems to have been that they had a reddish-brown skin, and black hair."

Meanwhile there was talk in London of how much money it had cost to fight the war against the French. Who should pay for it? The people in England were already heavily taxed. They reasoned that it was the colonists who most benefited from the victory, and they should be taxed to pay for it.

In November 1764, Franklin left for England to represent the people of Pennsylvania. Shortly after he arrived, the British Parliament in 1765 passed the Stamp Act. Colonists were required to buy stamps and affix them on all printed matter—on newspapers, almanacs, deeds, and playing cards. The money from the stamps was to go to England to help pay for the defense of the colonies.

Franklin, at first, was not against the tax, but there was great opposition in the colonies. No colonist was a member of the English Parliament where taxes and laws governing the colonies were passed. Colonists cried, ''Taxation without representation is tyranny.'' Franklin's attitude changed and he spoke in Parliament against the Stamp Act. It was repealed in 1766. In 1767, however, the English passed the Townshend Acts, a new tax on lead, paper, and tea. Franklin spoke out against these taxes, too. He called them ''acts of oppression.''

Benjamin Franklin felt the colonies were firmly set on the path to revolution. He tried to calm tempers in America and in England, to the point that people in both countries lost trust in him. In the colonies he was considered ''too much an Englishman.'' In London he was considered, ''too much an American.''

In England the feelings were especially bitter against Franklin after American patriots, protesting the tax on tea, on the night of December 16, 1773, dumped a few hundred chests of tea into Boston Harbor. Soon afterward, in 1774, the king removed Franklin as postmaster general of the colonies.

Benjamin Franklin left London in March 1775, and arrived in Philadelphia on May 5, 1775. During the years he had been away, his wife, Deborah, had died. Their daughter, Sarah, had married a young man Franklin had never met. And while he was at sea, on April 19, 1775, the first shots of the revolution were fired at Lexington and Concord.

The day after Franklin's return to the colonies, he was elected as a delegate to the Second Continental Congress. At sixty-nine, he was the oldest delegate.

The months ahead were busy ones for Franklin. He was re-named postmaster general, the first one in the new United States. (He gave his salary as postmaster to help wounded soldiers.) He proposed articles of confederation to unite the colonies and even traveled to Montreal to try and convince Canada to join the union. He was on the committee that drafted the Declaration of Independence. Franklin made a few suggestions to Thomas Jefferson who wrote the Declaration.

The colonies were fighting for their independence against the mightiest military power of the time. They needed help. In October 1776, Benjamin Franklin, along with diplomats Silas Deane from Connecticut and Arthur Lee from Virginia, sailed to France to try and convince the French to join the colonies in the fight against England.

The French people knew all about Benjamin Franklin, his writing and his scientific experiments. They gave him a great welcome. There were busts, rings, boxes, prints, and paintings all made to honor him. Franklin wrote to his daughter that in France his face was "as well known as that of the moon."

Franklin dressed plainly with a fur cap pushed down on his head, almost to his eyeglasses. It hid the eczema, an unpleasant-looking skin condition, on his scalp. Some Frenchwomen began wearing wigs in a fashion they called, *à la Franklin.* They were styled in the shape of his fur cap.

Franklin was especially popular with the women in France. They called him "Papa." Madame Brillon de Jouy wrote poetry and played music for him. He explained science to Marie Antoinette and played chess with the Duchesse de Bourbon. He proposed marriage to the beautiful Madame Helvétius. She refused.

Franklin's mission to France was a great success. Soon after he arrived, France began to secretly send guns, ammunition, and other provisions to the revolutionary army. French volunteers also went to America to help fight the British. In February 1778, the French signed a treaty with the United States to trade goods and to help the revolution. In September, the Continental Congress elected Franklin as the first United States minister to France.

On October 19, 1781, the revolutionary army, with the help of the French, won a great victory over the British in Yorktown, Virginia. American independence was considered won. In 1782, Franklin, with John Jay, who had been president of the Continental Congress and would be the first chief justice of the Supreme Court, and John Adams, who had been a member of the Continental Congress and would be the second president of the United States, negotiated peace with England. The Treaty of Paris was signed on September 3, 1783. The former thirteen colonies of England were now free and independent.

People in Europe were curious about the newly independent United States. What sort of country was it? Before Franklin left

Europe, he wrote, "The truth is, that though there are in that country few people so miserable as the poor of Europe, there are also very few that in Europe would be called rich . . . America is the land of the laborer . . . Our country offers to strangers nothing but a good climate, fertile soil, wholesome air, free government, wise laws, liberty, a good people to live among, and a hearty welcome."

6. *A Dying Man Can Do Nothing Easy*

BENJAMIN FRANKLIN left France in July 1785. A long line of mules carried the boxes of the many possessions he had acquired during his stay in France. People lined the roads to cheer him and say their good-byes. King Louis XVI sent Franklin a gift, a miniature portrait of the king in a frame set with more than four hundred diamonds.

Even at the age of seventy-nine, Franklin was still curious, still fascinated, by the world around him. On the sea voyage home, he measured the temperature of the ocean water at different depths. He noted the currents. He made a long list of suggestions for safer sailing.

Franklin arrived in Philadelphia on September 12, 1785. He was greeted with cheers and speeches, and cannons were fired in his honor. General George Washington sent him a letter of welcome. In his journal, Franklin wrote, "God be praised and thanked for His mercies."

Franklin was elected president of the Supreme Executive Council of Pennsylvania, a post similar to governor. The new federal government, with thirteen independent states, was not working well. A strong central government was needed. In 1787 a Constitutional Convention was called and Franklin was named a delegate.

Franklin did not agree with everything in the Constitution, but in his final speech to the convention, he said that the older he got, the more he doubted his own judgment. He encouraged those delegates with remaining objections to the Constitution to ''doubt a little of his own infallibility,'' and to ''put his name on this instrument.''

At one time Franklin owned slaves, but as early as 1751 he spoke out against slavery. In 1787 he was elected president of the first antislavery society in America, the Pennsylvania Society for Promoting the Abolition of Slavery, and the Relief of Negroes Unlawfully Held in Bondage. During his last years he wrote letters to newspapers and essays attacking slavery and the horror of making "traffic in the persons of our fellow men."

Benjamin Franklin had not lost his love for reading. In his house on Market Street in Philadelphia he had collected some four thousand books. His was one of the largest and best libraries in the country.

In the fall of 1789, Benjamin became quite ill and weak. He told his friends, "These pains will soon be over." He was dying and he knew it. On April 17, 1790, he asked his daughter to please change his sheets. He told her he wished to die "in a decent manner." He had difficulty breathing and someone at his bedside advised him to turn a bit so the breathing would come easier. Franklin said, "A dying man can do nothing easy." Those were his last words. He died that night. His daughter Sarah and seven grandchildren were with him.

Throughout the country and in Europe, people mourned his death. The French National Assembly set a three-month period of national mourning.

Benjamin Franklin was one of the greatest, most-loved Americans. His portrait has appeared on stamps, coins, and paper currency. His name has been given to streets, schools, museums, villages, and even to a short-lived state in the western section of North Carolina. During his long life he was a great writer, scientist, inventor, and statesman, but his epitaph, the inscription on his gravestone, was written more than sixty years before his death. He wrote it himself in 1728 at the age of twenty-two. This is how he wanted to be remembered:

The Body of
B. Franklin Printer
(Like the cover of an old book
Its contents worn out
And stript of its lettering and Gilding)
Lies here, Food for Worms.
But the work shall not be lost,
For it will (as he believed) appear once more
In a new and more elegant Edition
Revised and corrected
By the Author.

INDEX

To Leora, Nechama, and Aviva

D.A.A.

Library of Congress Cataloging-in-Publication Data
Adler, David A.
Benjamin Franklin—printer, inventor, statesman : a first biography / by David A. Adler ; illustrated by Lyle Miller.
p.　cm.
Includes index.
Summary: Follows the life of the accomplished American who achieved greatness as a writer, scientist, inventor, and statesman.
ISBN 0-8234-0929-5
1. Franklin, Benjamin, 1706–1790—Juvenile literature. 2. Statesmen—United States—Biography—Juvenile literature.
3. Printers—United States—Biography—Juvenile literature. 4. Inventors—United States—Biography—Juvenile literature.
[1. Franklin, Benjamin, 1706–1790. 2. Statesmen. 3. Printers. 4. Scientists.] I. Miller, Lyle, 1950–　ill.
E302.6.F8A27　1992　91-28816　CIP　AC
973.3′092—dc20
[B]